To YOUR GREATNESS

By CATHERINE STAFFORD AND HOWARD GLASSER

HEART ART BY ANNE LABOVITZ

TO YOUR GREATNESS!

The day we first met, I looked into your eyes. My heart, skipping beats, grew three times its size. I saw straight into your soul through those beautiful, wide eyes. Your greatness resides there. It can't be disguised.

I treasure that day and the moment we met. The seeds of your greatness were already set.

You never cease to amaze me with all that you do. I promised that day that I'd keep cheering you. To your greatness!

"To your greatness" is a phrase
that can be said as a toast.
It's a way for adults to show
pride and to boast.

This message is for YOU. I reflect
what I see, honor choices you make
to be the best YOU you can be.

Your greatness was born.
It was in you at birth.

My reflections are intended to
grow feelings of worth.

Get ready to hear about the
greatness I see.

I don't take this job lightly.
It's a heart gift from me.

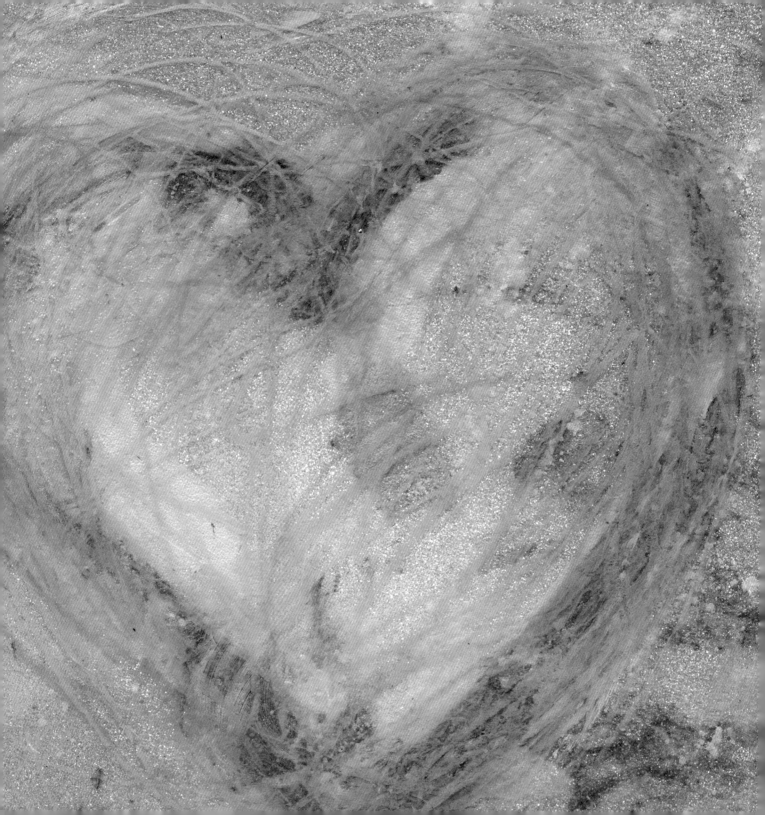

I may give you a wink with the words that I say. I may give a fist bump fifty times every day.

However I say it, whether quiet or loud, these reflections are shared to help YOU feel proud... of your greatness!

13

I first thought of greatness
as external, you see. I pictured
success, things I wished also
for me.

I dreamed of your greatness,
of what you would be, the things
you would do and the places
you'd see.

I NOW know that greatness is so very much more. Your greatness is who you are down to your core.

It's who you are as a friend, with compassion so true - what YOU give to the world, despite what it gives you.

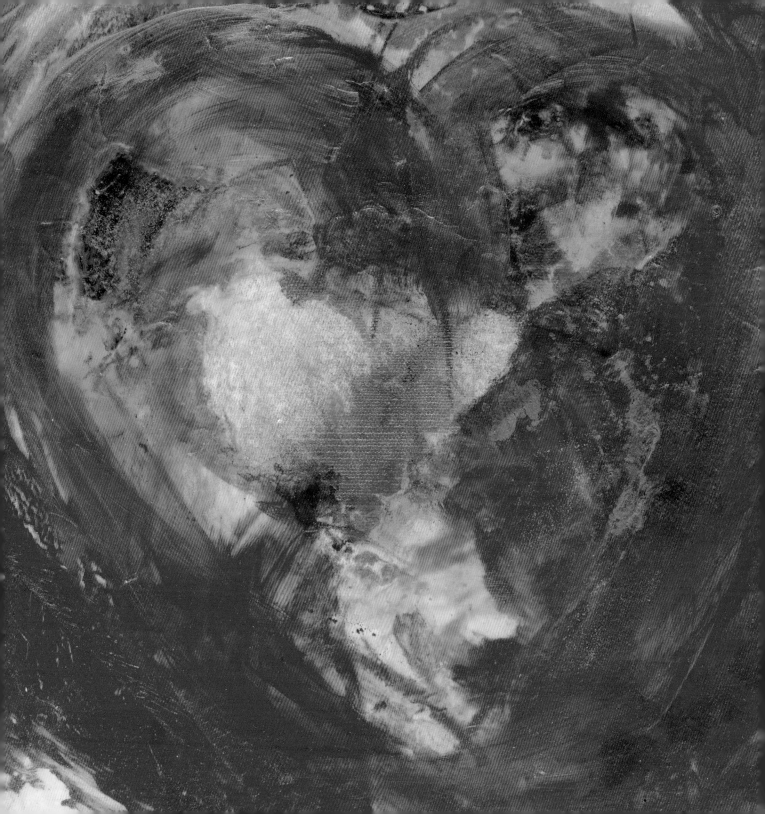

Your greatness resides deep in the depths of your heart. Your strengths and your gifts have been there from the start.

When I show appreciation, it's not just for what you DO. Your character and effort show much more about you.

Your tenacity and strength
overcome your life's stresses.
Your integrity and diligence push
you through your own messes.

You show up responsibly with
your family and school,
You're true to yourself, less
concerned about "cool."

21

If a $100 bill is all tattered and worn, its edges all faded and corners all torn, Its value is the same, despite where it's been, the way it's been used, or the shape that it's in.

It's the same with your greatness. It's your CORE inner worth. It's a gift from your Creator; you got it at birth.

You don't need to be perfect.
Just keep doing your best.
I can promise that life will push,
challenge and test... your true
greatness.

Challenging things will happen.
You'll want to rant and to rave.
Your greatness will hold and guide
you in the way you behave.

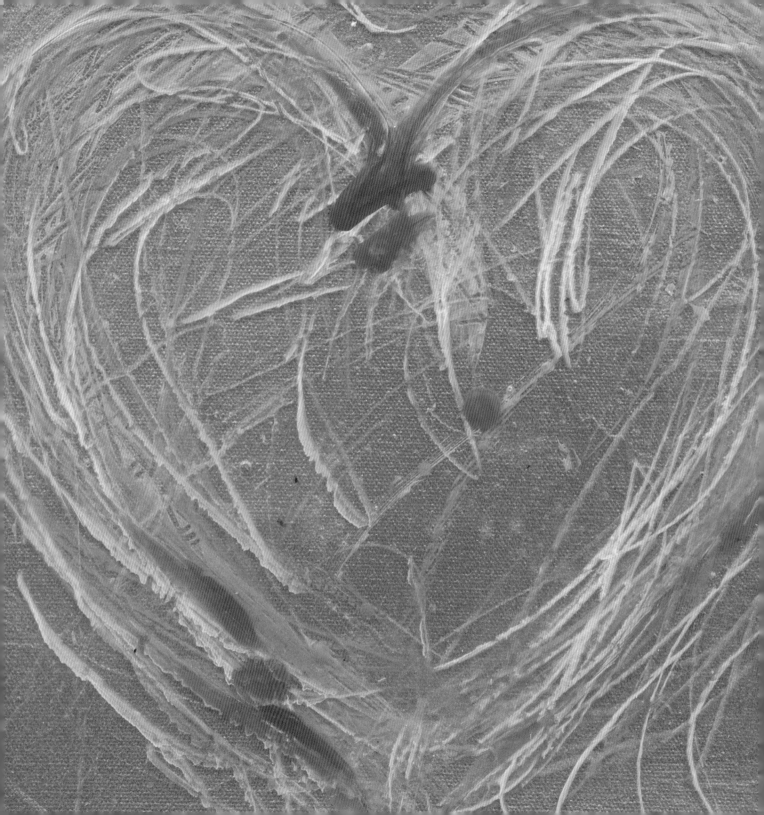

Just be who you are, your innermost self. Try not to get focused on status or wealth... That's not greatness.

It can be part of greatness - there's no doubt that is true. But remember, your greatness is more than what you do.

It's about what it TOOK to get where you are, the character you possess that will carry you far.

I see clever and witty, so much beyond "smart." Your brain skills balance with the gifts of your heart.

You are loving and kind, patient and just. To be in touch with THESE gifts is a true greatness must.

Greatness of compassion reflects back on you: doing for others what you'd have done to you.

To your greatness!

Feel your core gifts, given to you
at birth. It's HEART that defines
you and gives you your worth.

When I'm not with you and you
see a bright star, just think of
the light as my cheer from afar....
To your greatness!

Joyful Considerate Attentive COOPERATIVE A hard worker A source of
strength Courageous A LEADER Constructive A helper Committed Creative
GREAT EXAMPLE Courteous An advocate Aware DEDICATED TO SUCCESS DILIGENT
Discerning Direct Accomplished a lot CREATIVE Dignified Appreciative Easy
to like DEEPLY UNDERSTANDING A good friend Attentive to detail Productive
DEMONSTRATING Integrity exceeding expectations Gentle Inspiring
SURPRISING Efficient Empathetic Powerful WISE Faithful Brave Focused
BRINGING OUT THE BEST IN OTHERS Forgiving Generous Choosing what's important
COMPASSIONATE Gracious Going above and beyond Humility HONEST
Peacekeeper Genuine Glorious PRODUCTIVE Good-hearted Reasonable
Respectful HAVING UNIQUE IDEAS Resourceful Energetic Responsible RESPECTING
Self Reliable Enthusiastic Having great curiosity THANKFUL Self-controlled
Handling strong emotions well Inspiring SEEING THE BIG PICTURE Having an
open mind Honorable Having a positive attitude STRONG ON THE INSIDE
Hopeful Trustworthy Independent THOUGHTFUL Inquisitive Understanding
Intelligent JUST AND FAIR Kind Loving Using a pleasant voice
USING HIS GREAT MIND Vibrant Visionary Looking out for others MANAGING TIME
WELL A quick mind Making great choices Brilliant thoughts MAKING A GREAT
GUESS Organized Patient A great sense of humor LOGICAL Pulling together
Amazing forethought ENTHUSIASTIC Excellent planning skills Teamwork
MODEST Tenacious Responsible Deliberate SHOWING CHARACTER Joyful
Considerate Attentive COOPERATIVE A hard worker A source of strength

WHAT IS THE NURTURED HEART APPROACH?

The Nurtured Heart Approach is a way of awakening children to their greatness. Through three key stands, adults learn to see and express the beauty of everyday actions and choices. The approach helps build children's inner wealth and to use their intensity/life force in successful ways. While Howard Glasser originally developed the approach for highly challenging children, it has proven useful for facilitating parenting and classroom success for every child.

This approach's essence is in learning to express appreciation in profound ways while holding to a wonderfully easy, clear sense of limit-setting that does not accidentally convey to the child that the "gift of us" is most readily available in response to negativity.

The Nurtured Heart Approach has transformative impact even for children diagnosed with highly challenging behavioral or emotional symptoms – almost always without the need for long-term mental health treatment or medications. Even children experiencing social-cognitive challenges like autism and Asperger's benefit greatly from the approach. Its use with these populations reduces the need for traditional mental health and medical interventions.

NURTURED HEART APPROACH RESOURCES

Books and audio-visual resources listed below are available in most libraries and bookstores and from online sources. Phone orders can be made by calling our fulfillment
center, Brigham Distribution, at 435-723-6611.

BOOKS

Transforming the Difficult Child: The Nurtured Heart Approach (Revised 2013) by Howard Glasser and Jennifer Easley

All Children Flourishing – Igniting the Greatness of Our Children (2008) Howard Glasser with Melissa Lynn Block

Transforming the Difficult Child WORKBOOK – An Interactive Guide to the Nurtured Heart Approach (2013) Howard Glasser, Joann Bowdidge and Lisa Bravo.

ADHD Without Drugs – A Guide to the Natural Care of Children with ADHD (2010) Sanford Newmark, MD

Transforming the Difficult Child: True Stories of Triumph (2008) Howard Glasser and Jennifer Easley

Notching Up the Nurtured Heart Approach – The New Inner Wealth
Initiative for Educators (2011)
Howard Glasser and Melissa Lynn Block

Notching Up the Nurtured Heart Approach WORKBOOK
The New Inner Wealth Initiative for Educators (2011)
Howard Glasser and Melissa Lynn Block

AUDIO VISUAL RESOURCES

Transforming the Difficult Child DVD – (2004) 6 Hours
Based on an actual filmed one-day seminar – with video clip illustrations.

Transforming the Difficult Child DVD – (2004) 4 Hours
Based on an abbreviated version of the above.

Transforming the Difficult Child CD – (2011) 3.5 Hours
Recorded from a live seminar.

Transforming the Difficult Child: The Nurtured Heart Approach
Audio Book (2012)
Howard Glasser and Jennifer Easley – Read by Howard Glasser.

ONLINE CLASSES

Listings of classes on the Nurtured Heart Approach can be found
at www.ChildrensSuccessFoundation.com

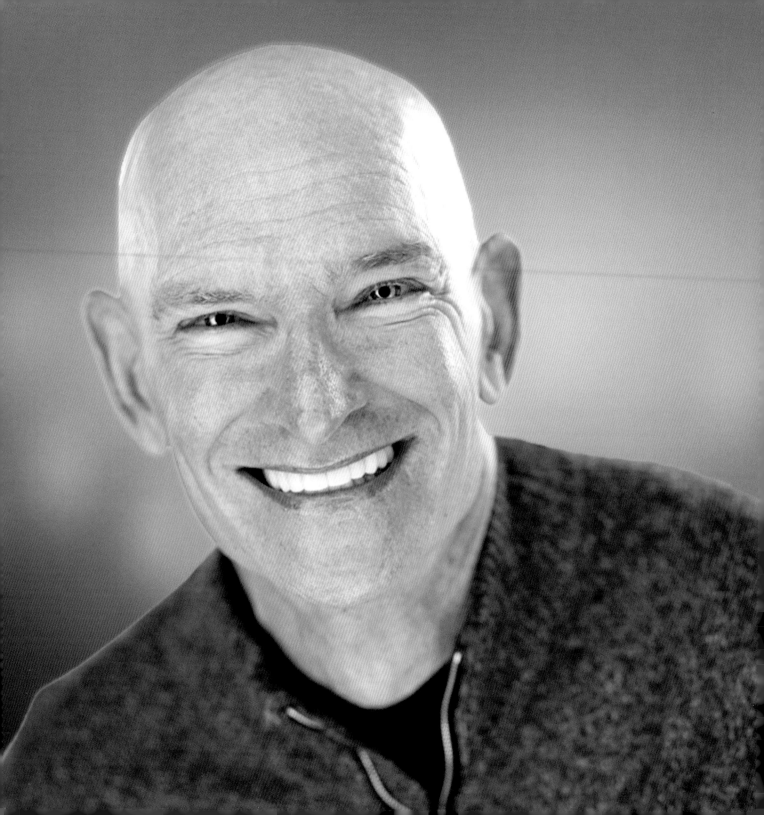

HOWARD GLASSER

Howard Glasser, creator of the Nurtured Heart Approach, is a psychotherapist, author, and Chairman of the Board of the Children's Success Foundation.

He has authored multiple books about the approach, including Transforming the Difficult Child, which remains a top seller in the ADHD category more than a decade after its initial publication.

Other titles include Notching Up the Nurtured Heart Approach: the New Inner Wealth Initiative (a leading book on school interventions) and All Children Flourishing (about using the NHA with all children, difficult or not. His most recent book, Igniting Greatness, is about applying the Approach to one's self as a way of transforming one's life and relationships.

When not writing and giving webinars from home, Howard spends much of his time on the road, traveling to cities worldwide to teach the Approach to parents, educators, therapists, and others who wish to make a dramatic difference in the lives of challenging children.

ANNE LABOVITZ

Anne Labovitz is a professional visual artist who lives and works in St. Paul, MN. Her practice includes painting, drawing, printmaking and public interventions as well as experimental film and sound. Labovitz has a degree in psychology and art from Hamline University in St. Paul.

Her work has appeared in solo and group exhibitions both domestically and internationally. Her paintings are included in the permanent collections at the Tweed Museum of Art in Duluth, the Athenaeum Music and Arts Library in La Jolla, CA, the Weisman Art Museum in Minneapolis, MN, the Minnesota Museum of American Art in St. Paul and in private collections worldwide. She has also co-authored and illustrated numerous books. Labovitz's latest project, 122 Conversations, commences in Thunder Bay, Canada 2015 and will travel through Sweden, Russia, Japan, and Iraqi Kurdistan, and will close in 2017 in Minnesota.

Labovitz's passion for people extends into her community involvement and her work teaching art to children, integrating her advanced training in the Nurtured Heart Approach (NHA). She presented at the NHA Global Summit in San Francisco in 2012. Several of her pieces in her Loving Heart series have been published on the cover of NHA books.

Labovitz's work is represented by the Burnet Gallery, Le Méridien Chambers, in Minneapolis.